بِسْمِ اللَّهِ الرَّحْمَٰنِ الرَّحِيمِ

In the Name of Allah, The All-Merciful,
The Kindest towards believers.

Disclaimer

All rights reserved. No part of this publication may be reproduced, stored in a retrieval system, or transmitted in any form or by any means, electronic, mechanical, photocopying, recording, or otherwise, without the prior written permission of the publisher, except in the case of brief quotations quoted in articles or reviews.

Contact : Admin@islamiclessonsmadeeasy.com.au

Visit us :
Facebook.com/islamiclessonsmadeeasy
Youtube.com/islamiclessonsmadeeasy
Instagram.com/islamic_lessons_me
Islamiclessonsmadeeasy.com.au
Ilme.net.au

The pictures used are the property of Islamic Lessons Made Easy. The content and rulings are taken from various leading scholars and are presented in a simplified manner. Therefore, for the exact definition and explanation, please refer to the original sources.

First Edition
©Copyright 2025 Islamic Lessons Made Easy

Contents

Transliteration — 4

Introduction — 5

Etiquettes of Qurān — 6

Sūrah al-Nās — 8

Summary — 24

Glossary — 34

Transliteration

ا	a	ق	q
ب	b	ك	k
ت	t	ل	l
ث	th	م	m
ج	j	ن	n
ح	ḥ	ه	h
خ	kh	و	w
د	d	ي	y
ذ	dh	ئ / آ / ـا	ā
ر	r	ـِي	ī
ز	z	ـُو	ū
س	s		
ش	sh		
ص	ṣ		
ض	ḍ		
ط	ṭ		
ظ	ẓ		
ع	ʿ		
غ	gh		
ف	f		

ء	Read with a sudden pause of air.
ﷺ	Blessings of Allah be upon him and his family.
عليها السلام	Peace be upon her.
عليه السلام	Peace be upon him.
سبحانه وتعالى	Glorious and Exalted Is He.

Introduction

Tafsīr is an Arabic word that means 'explanation'; it helps us understand what the verses of the Qurān really mean. Scholars study the Qurān by looking at its language, the history behind the verses and other aspects. They also think about how the verses were revealed and how we can use these teachings in our daily lives.

Tafsīr helps us connect with our faith and learn how to use the lessons of the Qurān today. It makes the wisdom of the Qurān easier to understand and more useful for us.

When we made this *Tafsīr*, we worked hard to gather ideas from trusted scholars and important books. We wanted to explain the Qurān in a way that is easy for you to understand.

We hope this *Tafsīr* helps you on your journey to learn more about the Qurān and your faith.

Etiquettes of Qurān

Before reciting, it is recommended to say:

أَعُوذُ بِاللَّهِ مِنَ الشَّيْطَانِ الرَّجِيمِ

A'ūdhu billāhi minash shayṭānir rajīm

I seek refuge with Allah from the accursed devil.

Then say:

بِسْمِ اللَّهِ الرَّحْمَٰنِ الرَّحِيمِ

Bismillāhir Raḥmānir Raḥīm

In the name of Allah, The Most Gracious, The Most Merciful.

- Make sure you have performed *Wuḍū* before touching any verse of the Qurān
- When reading the Qurān, it is better to face the *Qiblah*
- Make sure that the place where the Qurān is read is free from impurities
- Don't put the Qurān on the ground or anywhere it might get dirty
- Don't place anything on top of the Qurān
- When you recite the Qurān, try to pronounce the words correctly
- Take time to reflect on what the verses mean

After finishing your recitation, say:

صَدَقَ اللهُ العَلِيُّ العَظِيمُ

Ṣadaq Allāhul 'Aliyyul 'Aẓīm

Allah, the Sublime, the Great, has spoken the truth.

Sūrah al-Nās

Sūrah al-Nās

Sūrah al-Nās is the last chapter of the Holy Qurān.

According to narrations, Sūrah al-Falaq and Sūrah al-Nās were revealed together.

The key difference between them is that in Sūrah al-Falaq, we ask Allah ﷻ for protection from external evils, while in Sūrah al-Nās, we ask Allah ﷻ for protection from internal and hidden evils.

The Holy Prophet ﷺ:

Whoever recites Sūrah al-Nās and Sūrah al-Falaq, it is as if they have recited all the books revealed to the divine prophets.

(Majmaʿ al-Bayān)

بِسْمِ اللَّهِ الرَّحْمَٰنِ الرَّحِيمِ

Bismillāhir Raḥmānir Raḥīm

In the Name of Allah, The Most Gracious,
The Most Merciful.

قُلْ أَعُوذُ بِرَبِّ النَّاسِ

Qul a-ūdhu bi-rabbin nās

Say: I seek protection with the Lord of all the people.

The word *Rabb* (رَبّ) means someone who takes care of us and helps us grow, just like a parent does.

Allah ﷻ is the true *Rabb* of all people. He feeds us, protects us and looks after us in every way.

مَلِكِ النَّاسِ

Malikin nās

The King of all the people.

When we think of a king, we usually picture someone who rules over a country.

But Allah ﷻ is the real King, not just of one place, but of the entire universe. He controls everything, from the stars to the smallest creatures and takes care of all of it.

إِلَهِ النَّاسِ

Ilāhin nās

The God of all the people.

We are asking Allah ﷺ to protect us using three of His special qualities:

Ar-Rabb (ٱلرَّبّ) — the One who takes care of us,
Al-Malik (ٱلْمَلِك) — the King of everything,
Al-Ilāh (ٱلْإِلٰهِ) — the only true God.

But what are we asking protection from?

The next verse will explain ...

مِن شَرِّ الْوَسْوَاسِ الْخَنَّاسِ

min sharril waswāsil khannās

From the evil of the retreating tempter.

The word *al-khannās* (اَلْخَنَّاس) refers to someone who hides and comes back repeatedly, and this describes Satan.

He tempts us to commit sins, then retreats and hides, only to return and try again.

This verse means we are seeking protection from Allah ﷻ against the evil tempter who runs and hides when Allah's names are mentioned.

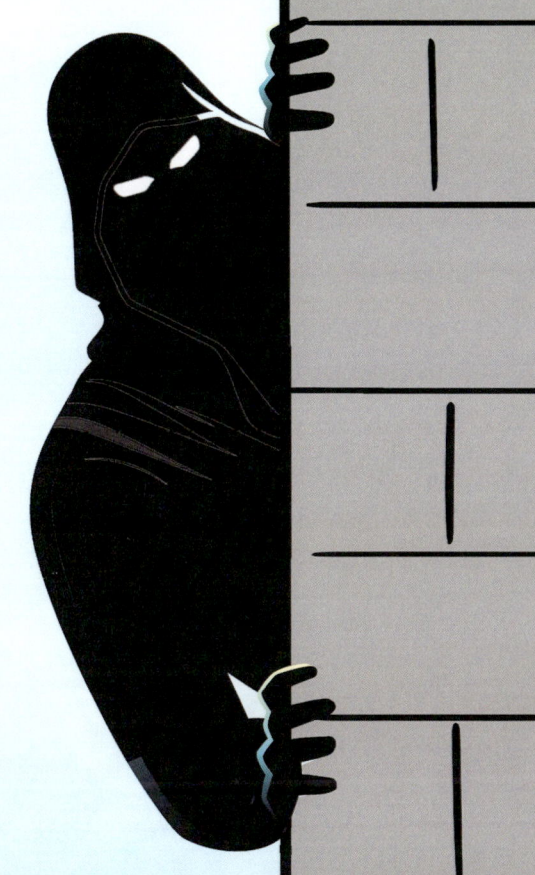

اَلَّذِي يُوَسْوِسُ فِي صُدُورِ النَّاسِ

alladhī yuwaswisu fī ṣudūrin nās

The one who tempts into the hearts of the people.

مِنَ الْجِنَّةِ وَ النَّاسِ

minal jinnati wan nās

From the Jinn and the people.

The Jinn (جِنّ) are another creation of Allah ﷻ, but we can't see them.

Some of them are good, while others do bad things.

So when we talk about *waswāsil khannās* (وَسْوَاسِ ٱلْخَنَّاسِ) — the sneaky temptations — they can come from both *Jinn* and people, trying to tempt us to do wrong.

Summary

From the start of this *Sūrah*, we are asking Allah ﷻ for help using three of His special qualities:

Ar-Rabb (ٱلرَّبّ) – the One who takes care of us,
Al-Malik (ٱلْمَلِك) – the King of everything,
Al-Ilāh (ٱلْإِلٰه) – the only true God.

Sometimes, *waswasa* (temptations) can make us forget these important qualities.

Sometimes, *waswasa* might make you think you are the real *Rabb*, as if you are the one who takes care of your kids, your garden or your house all by yourself.

Sometimes, *waswasa* might make you think you are the real *Malik*, making you feel like you are the king of your neighbourhood, your house or even your room.

Sometimes, *waswasa* might make you feel like you are an *Ilāh* or god.

But really, the only 'god' you are following is your desires, just like the Qurān says:

"Have you seen the one who takes his own desires as his god?"

(45:23)

When we ask Allah ﷻ for help in this *Sūrah*, and we say *Rabbin nās* (رَبِّ ٱلنَّاسِ), we are saying that we believe Allah ﷻ is the real Nurturer who takes care of us.

When we say *Malikin nās* (مَلِكِ ٱلنَّاسِ), we are saying we will obey Allah ﷻ, the true King in everything.

When we say *Ilāhin nās* (إِلَٰهِ ٱلنَّاسِ), we promise to worship Allah ﷻ alone, not ourselves or our desires.

A person who truly believes in these three qualities of Allah ﷻ will keep their ego in check and will be safe from the evil temptations of Satan, the Jinn and people who lead us into sin.

Glossary

Ilāh - God

Khannās - Retreater

Malik - King

Qiblah - Direction of the Ka'bah

Rabb - Nurturer

Sūrah - Chapter

Sūrah al-Falaq - Chapter of the Daybreak

Sūrah al-Nās - Chapter of the People

Waswasa - Temptations

Waswāsil khannās - Sneaky temptations

Credit

All praise belongs to Allah, the All Merciful towards all existents, the Kindest towards believers. He Who has given us enough patience and courage to complete this book.

Islamic Lessons Made Easy would like to thank all those involved in this project for their hard work and commitment.

CREATOR
Abbas Ibrahim

EDITORS
Kawthar Ibrahim
Sheikh Dr Zaid Alsalami

اللّٰهُمَّ صَلِّ عَلَى مُحَمَّدٍ وَآلِ مُحَمَّدٍ

Allahumma ṣalli ʿala Muḥammadi(n)w wa āli Muḥammad
O Allah, (please do) bless Muḥammad and the Household of Muḥammad

Contact: admin@islamiclessonsmadeeasy.com.au

Visit us:
Facebook.com/islamiclessonsmadeeasy
Youtube.com/islamiclessonsmadeeasy
Instagram.com/islamic_lessons_me
Islamiclessonsmadeeasy.com.au
Ilme.net.au

www.ingramcontent.com/pod-product-compliance
Lightning Source LLC
Chambersburg PA
CBRC091202070526
44583CB00008B/179